ONE PLANET LIVING

A SMALL INTRODUCTION TO A BIG IDEA: HOW WE CAN ALL ENJOY A HAPPY, HEALTHY LIFE WITHIN OUR FAIR SHARE OF THE EARTH'S RESOURCES

by Pooran Desai *and* Paul King
Foreword *by* Kevin McCloud

Written by Pooran Desai and Paul King

Additional writing and research
Peter Denton and Simon McWhirter

Foreword by Kevin McCloud

Editor Rachel Fielding

Design The Bridgewater Book Company

Printed by Butler & Tanner, Frome, UK.

© 2006 Pooran Desai and Paul King
Foreword © 2006 Kevin McCloud

Published by Alastair Sawday Publishing
Co Ltd

The Old Farmyard, Yanley Lane,
Long Ashton, Bristol, BS41 9LR

Tel: +44 (0)1275 395430

UK distribution: Penguin UK, 80 Strand,
London

A catalogue record for this book is
available from the British Library

Pooran Desai and Paul King have
asserted their rights to be identified
as the authors of this work.

One Planet Living® is a registered
trade mark.

ISBN 10 1-90170-85-X

ISBN 13 978-1-901970-85-2

The publishers have made every effort
to ensure the accuracy of the information
in this book at the time of going to press.
However, they cannot accept any
responsibility for any loss, injury or
inconvenience resulting from the use
of information contained therein.

Paper and printing: We have sought the
lowest possible ecological footprint from
the production of this book, using super-
efficient machinery, vegetable inks
and high environmental standards and
printing on recycled paper, Cyclus Print
(100% post-consumer waste).
Our printer is ISO14001-registered.

Photography credits:

Front cover Getty Images
Inside images courtesy of:
Alamy, pages 40, 55 (centre and right), 65 (top
left), 70-71, 79 (top left and bottom right), 83
(bottom right), 116-7; Bill Dunster Architects,
BedZED PV and wind cowls
pages 6, 7, 27, 30 (bottom left), 31 (top right), 38
(inset), 41 (bottom right), 62 (top), 64, 69
(all), 80, 87, 88, 98, 99 (bottom left and right),
102 (top), 104, 106 (top), 108 (left), 120;
BioRegional Quintain, pages 127, 128; Butterfly
Conservation/Martin Warren: *Comma butterfly*
pages 2, 10, and *Pearl-bordered fritillary butterfly*
page 98, Corbis, pages 12, 38, 67, 79, 82-3, 94,
104-5, 108 (bottom right), 120, Craig Churchill,
Black redstart page 39 ; Divine Chocolate/
Charlotte Borger, *Ama Achiaa*, pages 96-7;
Ecotopia, *Grolsch glasses*, page 91; Ecotricity,
Turbine page 25; Alan Frith and Pitfield Brewery,
Shoreditch stout page 11; Dusty Gedge, *Barclays,
Canary Wharf* page 37; Getty Images, pages 35
(top left and bottom), 46,74, 115; Martyn Goddard,
G-Wiz in Pall Mall page 68; Jennie Hills/Science
Museum, *Lasagne circuit board*, page 81; iStock,
Hops, Combine harvester page 10, page 18;
JupiterImages Corporation, pages 10 (bottom
right), 19 (top), 41 (top), 43, 45, 52, 56, 61, 72, 75,
84, 92, 95, 96, 100; Paul King, pages 50, 51;
Simon Lee, *Cyclotron Guitar* pages 102-3; London
Wildlife Trust's Centre for Wildlife Gardening,
Peckham, page 36; Marcus Lyon, *Pooran Desai*
page 30; NASA, pages 7, 14, 15, 17, 29, 49, 73, 93,
109, 124; PLI Designs, *Re-form chair* page 103;
Renewable Energy Systems Ltd/Fusion, *Aerial
view* page 26; RES/Peter Mackinven (bottom)
page 26; Edward Parker, *Charcoal in hands*,
page 99, reddot design, *Porsche Bike FS*
pages 62-3; Sheepdrove Organic Farm, pages
58-9; Sloeberry Trading, *Geetie Singh* page 11;
Smart Moves, page 65 (bottom right); Barbara
Strnadova, Silver Wing Creations page 34;
Warwick University, *Sunflower phone* pages 3,
85; WaterAid/Jon Spaull, page 55 (left), Michael
Whitehead, pages 47, 60, Paul Willatts, *Girl in
lavender field* pages 77-8, WWF, pages 20-21, 33
(top and bottom right), 107, 110, 111.

CONTENTS

Foreword *by Kevin McCloud*

Time was, long ago, in about 1980, eco-friendly living was a decidedly fringe activity for people with fringes. These were 'ecomentalists' who knitted their own socks from organic porridge, socks they then proudly displayed in sandals that they wore in December. They grew their own furniture and heated their homes with shared bodily warmth. In essence, then, these were people living not much differently from their 14th-century ancestors who sewed themselves into their underwear every autumn having first liberally rubbed themselves all over with goose fat.

But time, mercifully, has moved on. To be green in the 21st century no longer means you have to be alternative. The authors of this book wear ties and proper shoes in December and shave more often than I do. And the One Planet Living campaign they've devised is about incorporating affordable, small but meaningful strategies into your life. Strategies that don't involve living like a medieval serf. Strategies that (and this is important) can actually *improve* the quality of your life *and* make a meaningful contribution towards the reduction of CO_2 and the sparing of the world's resources.

Because, make no mistake, we are using the planet's raw materials, its water, minerals, metals and fuels at an unsustainable rate (you'll read plenty here to substantiate that). With the advent of global trade we have even come to stop valuing the human labour and energy that goes into making our world. And in losing all understanding of the value of things, and of the care that goes into creating them, we stop being a civilised and enriched society and become a market of throwaway consumers.

So if, like me, you despair of ever rising from the mire of materialism, stop reading your credit card bills and read this enjoyable book. It breaks sustainable living into chunks that you can understand and adopt just by making small changes to everyday decisions. It's a signpost to living within the planet's means.

But I think it's also a rallying cry for the reintroduction of some ideas that we haven't cherished for decades, perhaps centuries. Ideas such as respect for the material world around us, both man-made and natural. Which is why, among the guidelines about how to save water with aerated taps or reduce your holiday carbon footprint, there are also sections about buying Fairtrade goods and buying local or regional produce. Things you can do that go beyond the basic eco-mantra of 'reduce, re-use and recycle' and which are part of a wider ethical position. These ideas aren't radical; they haven't got greasy unwashed hair. They're just sensible and thoughtful and expedient. And in practice they can make our lives more rewarding and satisfying. More civilised.

INTRODUCTION

One Planet Living (OPL) is for everyone - including you.
It builds on the work of many individuals and organisations throughout the world
who have dedicated themselves to creating solutions to the environmental
challenges which face us. Two environmental organisations - BioRegional and WWF
- have come together to promote a simple set of principles which can make
sustainable living (living within the capacity of the planet without compromising
the needs of future generations) easy, attractive and affordable, not just here in
the UK but throughout the world.

You can start to apply these principles, these ideas, to your everyday life... today!
And to complement your efforts, BioRegional and WWF are working to build a
worldwide network of One Planet Living communities designed, among other
things, to be run completely on renewable energy.

We're also working with business to promote products and services which will help you lead a One Planet Lifestyle; we'll lobby government to remove barriers to sustainable living and to protect nature, and we'll promote public awareness of One Planet Living. All this will help improve our quality of life as well as contribute to the health of the planet by reducing our 'Ecological Footprint'.

And it's this Ecological Footprint which is at the heart of OPL. This timely invention measures the impact each of us makes on the planet. It works out how much land and sea is needed to feed us and provide all the energy, water and materials we use in our everyday lives. It also calculates the emissions generated from the oil, coal and gas we burn at ever-increasing rates, and it estimates how much land is needed to absorb all the waste we create (and there's plenty of it!).

But why is our footprint so important? Well, with more than six billion people living on the planet – and the number is increasing by 215,000 a *day* – each one of us needs to understand how much of the Earth's natural resources are available to share between us.

The ecological footprint information given throughout this book is only approximate. To find out more go to www.ecologicalbudget.org.uk.

8

Everything we do adds to the size of our footprint. Take, for example, the perfectly ordinary pastime of enjoying a beer. Just think for a moment... before you raised that drink to your lips, land was needed for growing the barley, for the brewery's operations, and for the pub, bar, restaurant or supermarket which sells the end product. And somewhere on the planet, more land was mined to make the metal for the combine harvester, the delivery truck and, finally, the can that was served to you. Now think about the number of beers that are sold in the world every day, and you begin to see the scale of the problem.

One answer, of course, is to go for a locally produced organic beer served in a bottle returned to the brewery for re-use. Impossible? Read on...

CHEERS, MINE'S AN ORGANIC!

Fancy a drink at the end of the day? Then why not go for a 'green' beer? In 1998, Geetie Singh revitalised the then-derelict Duke of Cambridge pub in Islington, north London, by turning it into the world's first certified organic pub. This eco-friendly local offers a range of organic beer, lager and wine including the specially brewed Shoreditch Stout from Pitfield Brewery and Freedom, the first organic draught lager available in the UK - reducing those all-important beer miles. As much of the daily organic menu as possible is sourced locally - bread, pickles and ice-cream are home-made and air freight is never used.

If we convert the food, materials and energy we consume into areas of land and sea required to produce them, we'd discover that for every tonne of paper we use each year, we need an area of forest about the size of five football pitches to produce it. And for each tonne of fish we eat, we need a sea area covering as much as 60 football pitches.

Satellite imaging tells us we have about 10 million square kilometres of cropland (that's an area a little bigger than China - two and a half billion football pitches), 40 million square kilometres of grazing land (five times the size of Australia), 30 million square kilometres of forest (more than twice the area of Antarctica) and 30 million square kilometres of fishing grounds. That sounds vast to ordinary mortals, but it's not if we have to support everyone on the planet.

The total works out at 110 million square kilometres of productive land and sea - about a quarter of the planet's total surface area (the rest is desert, deep ocean and high mountains, which are unproductive in terms of meeting our everyday needs, though of course valuable in other ways).

Every two years, WWF publishes a Living Planet report, which monitors the Earth's natural resources and how we use them. The latest report shows that we're consuming about 20% more each year than the planet can sustain into the long term. We're eating into the Earth's natural reserves by destroying our forests, over-fishing our seas and using farming techniques that exhaust the fertility of our soil that's been built up over centuries.

Mankind's global footprint is two and a half times larger than it was in 1961. As you might expect, there are large differences between the footprints of people in different countries: the average North American's, for example, is double that of someone in the UK and *seven* times that of the average African or Asian. The smallest footprints are made by impoverished countries such as Afghanistan and Eritrea.

This misuse of the Earth's natural resources can't go on. The fact is, if everyone on Earth consumed as much as the average person here in the UK, we'd need *three* planets to support us – and if we consumed as much as the average American, we'd need *six* planets.

Which is where One Planet Living comes in.

It's now essential that One Planet Living become the norm around the world – and that it's attractive and affordable. It must address everyday concerns about our homes, our clothes, food, health, education and leisure, as well as energy and transport.

OPL (as we shall now call it) must also be straightforward. It's easy to make everyday decisions that have damaging consequences, particularly to the environment, but OPL is here to show how the sustainable options – which have a positive impact on our health, those around us and our planet – can be simple and straightforward, too.

One Planet Living aims for...

- Zero carbon
- Zero waste
- Sustainable transport
- Sustainable materials
- Local and sustainable food
- Sustainable water
- Natural habitats and wildlife
- Culture and heritage
- Equity and fair trade
- Health and happiness

These aims or principles aren't in any particular order – they're all important and they're all interconnected. We'll take them one by one in the following pages, and show how you can adopt and adapt them to your everyday life. And it's easy – because it's largely to do with common sense.

So how do we begin to 'go green'? And with such a wealth of information around, how do we know what's right, what's wrong... and what's just plain daft?

After all, more and more companies are offering greener products and services these days, and the information they publish can sometimes be contradictory. As every day passes, the latest technology is offering us new solutions. And what about the choices we have to make... for example, is it better to buy organic tomatoes from overseas, or non-organic ones that have been grown locally? (The answer, of course, is local organic!)

So the first step is... be aware. (The fact that you're reading these words shows that you're exactly that!) It's not going to be long now before One Planet Living will be second nature and part of your everyday life!

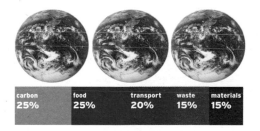

| carbon 25% | food 25% | transport 20% | waste 15% | materials 15% |

ZERO CARBON

Be energy-efficient at home and at work – and sign up to green power

Every time you turn on a light switch, use a computer, watch television or cook a meal, the chances are you're creating carbon dioxide – CO_2.

CO_2 is a prime polluter of the environment – and *the* prime contributor to global warming. We create it whenever we burn fossil fuels such as coal, oil and natural gas (called fossil fuels because they have been created over millions of years by the slow underground transformation of vegetation and other living matter).

Scientists believe that global average temperatures could rise between 1.4°C and 5.8°C by 2100 – that's probably in our grandchildren's lifetime. This increase may not seem significant to the average person – but it's *hugely* significant to the planet and, therefore, to all our lives.

Indeed, that kind of temperature rise will affect our weather patterns and sea levels. Glaciers are already melting in places as far apart as Australasia and Switzerland, snow is receding from the peaks of the great mountain ranges, shorelines are eroding and great natural events such as hurricanes, storms and flooding are on the increase. People are being affected everywhere - from Boscastle to Bangladesh and New Orleans to New Zealand - and wildlife and their habitats are also under threat.

Climate change, then, is the urgent issue. To tackle it, we will need to wean ourselves off our dependence on the fossil fuels we use to run our transport and heat and power our homes and offices.

WHAT CAUSES GLOBAL WARMING?

The Earth's climate is driven by energy from the sun. The sun warms the Earth's surface, but as the temperature increases, the Earth reflects this energy back into space. Some is absorbed by naturally occurring gases in the atmosphere such as methane, CO_2 and nitrous oxide. But over the decades, as a result of human activities, these gases have built up to form a blanket around the Earth - and as each year passes, they trap more and more heat that would otherwise escape into space. This creates what is commonly called the 'greenhouse effect'. Carbon dioxide is the most significant of these gases - and the more of it we emit, the thicker the ethereal blanket becomes, and the more the planet warms up.

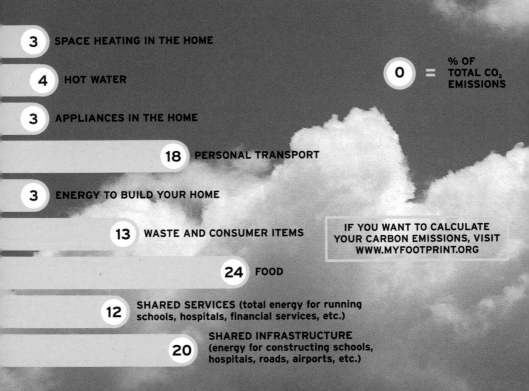

WHERE DO CARBON EMISSIONS COME FROM?

Your CO$_2$ emissions will depend a lot on where and how you live. For example, a person living in a new, well-insulated home, driving 5,000 miles a year and taking one short-haul flight per year, will be responsible for about 12 tonnes of CO$_2$ per year

3 SPACE HEATING IN THE HOME

4 HOT WATER

0 = % OF TOTAL CO$_2$ EMISSIONS

3 APPLIANCES IN THE HOME

18 PERSONAL TRANSPORT

3 ENERGY TO BUILD YOUR HOME

13 WASTE AND CONSUMER ITEMS

IF YOU WANT TO CALCULATE YOUR CARBON EMISSIONS, VISIT WWW.MYFOOTPRINT.ORG

24 FOOD

12 SHARED SERVICES (total energy for running schools, hospitals, financial services, etc.)

20 SHARED INFRASTRUCTURE (energy for constructing schools, hospitals, roads, airports, etc.)

One way we can do this is to cut down on the amount of energy we use - and if you think about it for a moment, that's a pretty easy thing to do. Some of the biggest savings come from very simple things:

- Using energy-efficient lightbulbs.

- Switching off lights and computers when we're not using them.

- Turning the thermostat down by just 1°C.

- Boiling only as much water as we need for a cup of tea or a pan of vegetables.

- Insulating the hot water tank, loft and walls, and draught-proofing windows and doors.

You'll probably be as surprised as we were to discover that just simple everyday actions like these can reduce electrical energy consumption by as much as a *third*.

Thinking of buying a new fridge, or perhaps a washing machine or dishwasher? These days, many electrical products carry a label which tells you how energy-efficient they are. So why not opt for the most efficient appliance which also fits in with your other priorities such as style and colour? You'd be doing yourself, your bank balance *and* the planet a huge long-term favour!

SAVE ENERGY

Of course, not everything is yet clearly labelled - televisions, for instance. So ask about their power rating (LCD televisions are generally more efficient than traditional cathode ray tubes and plasma screens, by the way). Remember also that water-efficient washing machines and dishwashers can also save energy by reducing the amount of hot water used. As indeed can spray taps and 'entrained air showers', which suck in air to bulk out the water. (A modern entrained air shower is great to use - and only consumes half as much water as a power shower.)

Another way of cutting back on fossil fuel use is to make sure that more of the energy we consume comes from renewable sources such as wind, wave and solar power, and biomass (such as wood from sustainably managed forests or farmland).

All electricity supply companies in the UK are now required by government to source a growing percentage of their electricity from renewable sources, which means that consumers have the choice of 'green' tariffs. Solar hot water units have come down in price, and are being installed as a matter of course in more and more buildings, new and old, across the country. Small wind turbines, too, are gradually becoming available. Woodchip and wood pellet stoves are also a good alternative to coal and oil burners. And these days, blocks of flats can be fitted with Combined Heat and Power (CHP) systems, which generate electricity and use the heat that's created to provide hot water.

CARBON-FREE OVALTINE!

With just a little bit of foresight and application, even ages-old buildings can be rehabilitated so that carbon dioxide emissions can  be eliminated altogether. The historic Ovaltine factory at Beaufort Court, Kings Langley, Hertfordshire, has been transformed by an international wind farm developer, Renewable Energy Systems, into the first commercial zero CO_2 emissions building in the world.

The 1930s-built Ovaltine Egg Farm, which housed the 50,000 chickens that laid the eggs for the famous malt drink, is entirely energy self-sufficient. Power is provided by a wind turbine, special solar panels which generate heat and electricity, grasses that are grown to act as energy crops, an underground heat store and a groundwater system which cools the offices and feeds excess water back into the grass crop for irrigation. Any additional power created on-site is sold to the National Grid.

CHP is so efficient that even if it uses a fossil fuel such as natural gas, it can still reduce CO_2 emissions by about 30%. CHP can provide energy for anything from an individual home to an entire community. Some CHP systems can run on renewable fuels such as wood.

And so from home to work. Generally speaking, the same energy tips apply there, as well. We're already well used to power-saving computer screens, but these days even large photocopiers can be energy-efficient. And here's a thought... what about suggesting your company generates its own renewable energy? Just as for

domestic use, solar hot water systems are available to businesses throughout the country, as are small electricity-generating wind turbines and solar panels that generate electricity.

All companies – including the one *you* work for – can benefit from being more energy-efficient. In the long run, this efficiency saves them money, boosts their profits, increases their employees' job security... and helps the planet. Everyone's a winner!

The nuclear option

Nuclear power. It's the hot topic of the day, and with good reason – will the UK increase its nuclear capacity, or invest far more in increased energy efficiency and the huge potential of renewable energy?

There are 443 nuclear power stations in the world today, including 12 operating in the UK. Together, they provide up to 7% of the world's energy and 17% of its electricity. Because of huge increases in the price of oil, continuing instability in the Middle East and international commitments to reducing CO_2 emissions under the Kyoto Protocol, the 'nuclear option' is being vigorously debated.

On one side is the 'low-carbon emissions' argument; on the other, environmental engineers and Non-governmental organisations point to other low-carbon energy sources which don't have the associated risks relating to storage, security and contamination. Such risks, the NGOs say, are too serious and dangerous to contemplate. This is not to mention the massive costs associated with nuclear power generation and the unresolved question of how to deal with the radioactive waste products.

Then there's the question of the world's rapidly depleting supplies of uranium which won't last for ever because they're finite and can't be renewed. Far better then to reduce our energy demand and invest in renewables.

Depending on what you use at home, and on whether you live in an old or new home, energy contributes up to about 15% of your Ecological Footprint. Energy used at work, at school and in hospitals adds another 10%. But through long-term energy efficiency and the use of renewable energy, we can set a target to reduce our energy footprint to almost zero. How can this be done? Well... asking your energy provider for green electricity and...

- Fitting your home with energy-saving systems – loft insulation, for example – can reduce your heating footprint (and your bills) substantially. By simply replacing normal bulbs with the energy-efficient kind, you use 70% less energy for lighting.

- Turning down your thermostat by only 1°C could reduce your energy consumption for heating by 10%.

AN URBANE STYLE OF LIVING

When Pooran Desai helped start BioRegional in 1994 with his partner, Sue Riddlestone, little did they imagine that a few years later they'd be living and working in their own eco-village in South London.

Here we are, leading a greener lifestyle at BedZED - the Beddington Zero (fossil) Energy Development. Even though it's a high-density development, most homes have a garden - mine's a roof garden overlooking the village square. South-facing conservatories mean we can collect heat from the sun and solar panels generate

electricity. The brightly coloured wind cowls on top of the development have become an iconic feature, known by everyone for miles around - but they're an essential part of the natural ventilation system we all enjoy. The topmost roofs are

covered in a mat of flowering sedum plants. We have a well-used and popular car club at BedZED. Three cars are conveniently on site and I never have trouble getting one when I need it. Admittedly, for the odd weekend jaunt in summer, I do have a sports car - but it's a 'zero carbon zero waste' car which runs on waste cooking oil, and I love it!

Leave space for your local wildlife – it's declining faster than you imagine

Do you know who your neighbours are?

No, not the people next door, but those *other* neighbours... the hedgehogs, robins, newts, bats, owls, frogs and so on.

The UK is blessed with a wonderful array of wildlife and, depending on where you live, your natural neighbour could be anything from a dolphin to a grass snake. And just think of our habitats... wetlands, peat bogs, meadows, rolling downs, chalk rivers, peaks, hills and dales. And, of course, we're surrounded by the sea.

The trouble is that pollution and other environmental hazards are taking their toll. If we want our wild species and spaces to thrive, we must do whatever we can to protect them.

Great crested newt

All life on Earth depends on how we use the planet's renewable and non-renewable resources – which is the ultimate reason why OPL is so important. Everything in the natural world is interconnected, and we interfere with it at our peril: destroying a rainforest, for example, not only has a profound effect on species ranging from the orang-utan to the Hewitson's blue hairstreak butterfly (*see right*), it can also impinge on soil stability, which in turn can lead to flooding many kilometres away, and have a impact on global weather systems.

The Living Planet Report produced by WWF every two years shows that populations of terrestrial, freshwater and marine vertebrate species have declined by about 40% over the last 30 years.
So given that the state of biodiversity – the natural wealth of animal and plant species – affects us all, an alarming statistic like that should act as a real warning.

By supporting an environmental organisation, you can directly help endangered species and their habitats on a global scale. In addition, there's much we can do to help our *local* biodiversity, which is also hugely important. Some of our wildlife in the UK might not be as charismatic as the snow leopard, but it's still difficult not to

be thrilled by the sight of a kestrel hovering... or even a hedgehog scurrying across the lawn at dusk.

Happily, it's easy to encourage wildlife into our gardens (and make no mistake about their importance: they cover an incredible 2,700 square kilometres of UK prime land, according to the Royal Horticultural Society!) For a start, make yours a pesticide-free zone. Create a natural wilderness patch; maybe even dig a pond, which will reward you for years to come. You could sow some wild flower seeds - poppies and foxgloves make wonderful displays, for example - and start a compost heap.

While you're about it, put down a few stones or a log pile. Birds will enjoy them and small creatures such as frogs will use them for shelter and protection. And don't forget nesting boxes and feeders, either - and why not put up a bat box, too? Find out more from your local wildlife trust.

On a wider scale, it's also important that we help protect the habitats that surround us. Meadows are disappearing, rivers and streams are being polluted, peat bogs are under threat, the urban sprawl is spreading. One way of making a difference is to keep a sharp eye on local planning applications and make your views known to your MP and local council.

These days, responsible house-builders and other developers carry out ecological surveys before starting work on a site, so progress is being made. If we're buying a new home, we can ask whether it's been EcoHomes-rated - this rating, ranging from *excellent* to *pass*, indicates to what extent the developer has taken into account a range of green issues including the ecological value of the site and whether it has enhanced its wildlife value. Systems like this contribute directly to the environment, of course - and to your bank balance!

GARDENS WITH A VIEW

The Derry and Toms department store in Kensington started it all, way back in 1936. The company's vice-president had a revolutionary idea to create the world's first roof garden. When it opened to the public, it became a sensation and a unique tourist attraction.

The store has long since gone, but the garden remains. What's more, the last 10 years have seen a resurgence of interest in roof gardens in cities as far afield as Australia, Germany, Japan, Sweden and the United States.

The idea is simple - as the urban sprawl continues to sprawl and green land becomes ever more scarce, why not turn flat roofs into green havens for plants and wildlife?

A leading proponent of green roofs is Dusty Gedge, who has been campaigning and advising on the subject for 10 years. He has been one of the most influential figures in persuading the Canary Wharf management in London to create green roofs on their tower blocks, and in 2004 he won a British Environment and Media Award for his long-term efforts.

URBAN JUNGLE? NO, A SUSTAINABLE FOREST!

BioRegional and the London Borough of Croydon have been working together to put all the borough's street and park trees under a formal sustainable management plan. Not only has this increased the trees' value to wildlife in an urban area, it has enabled tree surgery waste to be processed into woodchip for supply to local energy-generating plants rather than sent to landfill, saving on both our waste and energy footprints - a double whammy. It also shows how

even urban areas can supply us with natural resources. Croydon is the only urban area to achieve international Forest Stewardship Council certification - which means that it's now classified as a well-managed forest!

FSC

Properly conducted land surveys enable developers to discover what already lives in or depends on a particular site, and to draw up a plan to maintain or enhance its ecological value. Some disused sites in big cities – 'brownfield' sites – have become important wildlife oases that are home to kestrels, butterflies, wild flowers and even more unusual birds such as the black redstart. The value of these urban patches can be huge – on occasion even

Black redstart

greater than that of some seemingly pristine 'greenfield' sites which, on closer inspection, may have been covered with pesticides for years. Brown or green, if such places *must* be developed, we can all play our part in ensuring that the development is sympathetic to local nature.

Then, of course, there's the even wider world, outside the UK. We can all do our bit to help conserve biodiversity overseas – for example, by buying timber or wood products that have been certified by the Forest Stewardship Council (*see Sustainable materials page 102*), and by selecting organic products which range from bed sheets to coffee beans.

LOCAL AND SUSTAINABLE FOOD

Go for local, seasonal and organic food – and enjoy the taste sensation!

Answer this truthfully... do you really *need* to eat strawberries in February? Or peas flown in from South Africa? Or plastic-wrapped parsley from the Middle East?

The answer's probably 'no' – and from an environmental perspective, it's *definitely* 'no'. Did you know, for example, that per mile, air freighting releases 10 times as much CO_2 into the atmosphere as goods transported by road, and 50 times more than sea freighting? Or that more energy is used in packaging many foods than in the food itself? You may also not realise that most of our imported lettuce comes from Spain, which also supplies us with hundreds of thousands of tonnes of tomatoes. Just imagine the quantities of water required to irrigate these crops in one of the driest countries in Europe.

Food makes up the largest part of our Ecological Footprint - in the UK it's about a quarter of the total. Globally, food statistics are amazing - for example, 70% of freshwater consumed worldwide is used for agriculture, and it can take up to 15,000 litres of water to produce 1kg of beef. Sitting down to a meal is a necessary and enjoyable experience, of course - but as we do so, let's consider the resources used not only to grow and process the food, but also how far it's come and how much of it was packaged.

Air freighting fresh produce has more than trebled in the past 20 years. It's now very big business indeed - but at what cost? To give you some idea, each tonne of strawberries we fly into the UK from, say, the Middle East releases more than four and a half tonnes of CO_2 - the principal cause of climate change. The same amount of strawberries produced and delivered locally and in season will release just 17 kg of CO_2 - roughly one three-hundredth of that amount!

Although we could meet over 70% of our eating needs, half of the food consumed in the UK is imported. What's more, we also move food between countries for no obviously good reason. For example, we import more than 100 million litres of milk from the Netherlands... and export double that amount to the same country! In one recent year, the UK also imported 240,000 tonnes of pork and exported 195,000 tonnes; and we imported 125,000 tonnes of lamb and exported 102,000 tonnes. Does this make sense?

One way of easily reducing the environmental burden of freight is to buy local produce – perhaps from one of the increasingly popular farmers' markets. Just this single gesture will support local jobs, help create a sense of community, keep some of those 40-tonne delivery trucks off the road for some of the time... and help repair our damaged planet. Many local markets are now certified by the National Association of Farmers Markets, so that you know that the produce on sale will have been grown, reared, caught, brewed, pickled, baked, smoked or processed by the stallholder.

Organic and other low-input forms of farming that use little or no pesticides or fertilisers consume up to 40% less energy in production and usually support higher levels of wildlife on the farms. Many people regard organic food as healthier because of issues such as pesticides, nitrates and genetic modification. Others are concerned about land quality and animal welfare, provision of wildlife habitats and, of course, the overall Ecological Footprint impact. Although often more expensive, organic food is coming down in price. Whenever possible, maximise the amount of seasonal produce you buy locally and there's nothing more sustainable, better tasting or fresh than home-grown fare from your own organic garden or allotment. Great exercise and a delicious result!

Home delivery is becoming more and more popular. An organic box of vegetables or a supermarket load delivered to your door... it all helps cut down on your car dependence. If you visit a supermarket weekly, try making it fortnightly instead. Ask your supermarket to stock more local produce - remember that managers (even supermarket managers!) are influenced by their customers. In buying a local organic box you will find that the food is less packaged and you can return the box for re-filling - saving on your waste footprint as well. Enjoy the strawberry, sweetcorn and turnip (!) seasons.

IN CLOVER IN GLOUCESTERSHIRE

The Prince of Wales' Duchy Home Farm at Highgrove shows how sustainable farming can support the goal of One Planet Living.

All the land is farmed organically and, unusually for a modern farm, it sustains a mix of agricultural enterprises which support each other ecologically and economically. These include a dairy herd, beef suckler cows, sheep, rare breed pigs - Tamworths and Large Blacks - arable crops and 50 acres of vegetables supplying organic wholesalers, local schools, supermarkets and vegetable box deliveries to 140 nearby families.

And the key to all this? The traditional wisdom of crop rotation... and clover. Fields of oats, wheat, rye and barley - and spring beans - are rotated with pasture sown with clover. This not only provides grazing, but also fixes nitrogen from the air into the soil, fertilising it naturally.

Oats and wheat grown on the farm are used to produce Duchy Original biscuits - with the profits going to The Prince's Charities Foundation.

Culture, heritage, sustainable farming, rural jobs and fair trade - it takes the biscuit!

Buying fish products with confidence

More than two billion people depend on fish as a source of animal protein – and some 200 million people earn all or part of their living from fishing activities. The United Nations estimates that humans now consume more than 100 million tonnes of fish every year – so much so that three quarters of the world's fishing grounds are over-exploited.

That's why WWF and Unilever, the world's largest buyer of seafood, established the Marine Stewardship Council (MSC) in 1997. Today, the MSC is an independent global non-profit organisation which has developed an environmental standard for sustainable and well-managed fisheries. Fish products bearing the MSC's eco-label are guaranteed to have come from a well-managed fishery and have not contributed to over-fishing.

Among the MSC-certified products, now widely available, are Thames herring, Hastings mackerel and herring, and prawns from Loch Torridon in Scotland. Other labelled products come from as far afield as Alaska, Mexico and Western Australia. Look out for the MSC eco-label in shops and supermarkets, and on restaurant menus.

We're not saying we should *only* eat local, organic and seasonal produce – but there's no reason why it can't make up half our diet. Much of the countryside we love has been shaped by farming the land over the centuries, so in buying local produce, we're supporting local employment *and* helping maintain our countryside as well – as some supporters of our countryside say, we can 'eat the view'.

A more localised food system has other benefits, too. Transporting livestock shorter distances is more humane, shows concern for their welfare and reduces the risk of diseases being spread (it's believed the foot and mouth disease epidemic in 2001 emanated from contaminated meat imported from Asia and eventually cost the UK around £9 billion – and the rural economy is still recovering.)

Having said all that, we mustn't overlook the importance of international trade, especially when it supports developing countries and when it's certified as fairly traded or backed by organisations such as the Rainforest Alliance, which sets standards for sustainable agriculture, wildlife and workers' rights (see also *Equity and fair trade page 95*). But let's go for delivery by sea rather than air. South Africa, for example, earns 20 times as much money for each tonne of CO_2 released from exporting sea-freighted Cape wines than for air-freighted grapes: a positive way of earning foreign exchange *and* minimising the damage to the environment.

And finally... here's a radical thought for the carnivores among us - go vegetarian for a day! Replace one meat meal a week with a vegetarian option. Because of the huge tracts of land used for raising, for example, beef, reducing the meat in your diet is a powerful way of reducing your Ecological Footprint - indeed, it might be a bigger saving than any other single dietary measure.

Food makes up 25% of the average person's Ecological Footprint. By starting a local and sustainable food plan, you can reduce your total Ecological Footprint by as much as 15%.

● **Eating more fruit and vegetables and less meat could reduce your food footprint by up to 40%.**

● **Buying produce locally could reduce your food footprint by around 10%.**

● **Buying more organic food can reduce your footprint by 15%.**

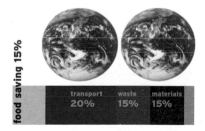

food saving 15%

| transport | waste | materials |
| 20% | 15% | 15% |

THE PLEASURE OF A VEGETABLE PATCH...

Paul King, his partner Gail and their two small children moved to Shropshire 18 months ago because they not only wanted a better, healthier life for themselves, but also because they were keen to get closer to a One Planet lifestyle. The home they moved to is part of a new development that was shortlisted for the WWF/House Builders Federation Sustainable Homes Award in 2004.

"There really is a huge amount of 'feel-good factor' in trying to lead a One Planet Lifestyle," says Paul. "Gail and our boys have had a huge amount of pleasure out of our vegetable patch, for example – and because what we're eating is home-grown, we've truly reconnected with the countryside and the changing seasons.

Although we're living in a rural area, I can easily work from home for a day or two a week thanks to broadband. I can get a lot more work done in the peace and quiet, than in a busy office. My 'sustainable home' feels good because it has big windows – which is great for natural light in winter as well as summer – and it's bright, warm, dry and quiet because of the high levels of recycled newspaper insulation and the triple glazing. Not only is this good for the planet, but our energy bills are a lot lower, too!

I'm proud of the fact that most of the timber in our house comes from certified, well-managed forests and that the bricks and roof tiles are reclaimed from buildings that have been demolished in the same part of the country. Something else that really works is having a segregated waste bin under the sink and a recycling point a few hundred metres from our

front door, so that less of our everyday rubbish adds to the growing landfill crisis.

Our move here is one of the best things we've done. We enjoy our new home and we're beginning to feel part of a wider community in our town. For us, the pursuit of One Planet Living is more happiness than hardship."

SUSTAINABLE WATER

Cutting back on water consumption is simpler than you think

Spend half an hour getting drenched in a downpour and you'll be hard-pressed to believe that the world is suffering from a water shortage.

This transparent, colourless, odourless and tasteless liquid compound that falls from the sky and gurgles from springs may *seem* to be infinite, but the truth is quite different. The planet's water supply is strictly limited – and as the human population continues to increase, so the usable water available to us is diminishing. According to WaterAid – the international charity which helps local communities set up low-cost sustainable projects to provide water – more than a billion people in the world today are denied access to safe water, and over two billion lack adequate sanitation.

Here in the UK, the use of water is a growing issue as our weather patterns are changing and our aquifers – vast underground reservoirs – are drying up.

Yet despite all that, what do we do with this incredible resource? We waste it and pollute it, we dump oil, chemicals, mercury and even cyanide into it. We build towns where water supplies are unsustainable and we divert rivers and destroy vital floodplains for agriculture. It's almost criminal (and in some cases it *is*).

It's time to cut back - because every drop counts.

The UK government is planning a major new programme of house-building in England over the next few years - but if we continue to use water as we're doing right now, it's more than likely that there simply won't be enough of it to supply all the new homes.

The good news is that it's now possible to install water-efficient appliances, including taps, showers and toilets, in new homes at no extra cost - good news because these measures alone can cut water usage by as much as 30%. And while the government isn't yet requiring house-builders to be water-conscious in this way, a brand new voluntary Code for Sustainable Homes is leading the way by encouraging builders to use much greater water and energy efficiency measures into all new homes.

Meanwhile, what can we all do?

Take a shower instead of a bath – or at least opt for a shallower bath. When you next install a new shower head or taps, ask for water-efficient sprays or those that mix air with the water rather than a power shower (that way, you'll use something like 50% less water).

Likewise the toilet, the washing machine, the dishwasher… it's now easy to make sure we get a water-efficient product.

Water costs money, of course, but what about our free supply from the heavens above? Simple things like water butts that collect rainwater from our drainpipes and guttering can radically reduce the amount of treated water we use to wash the car or water the garden.

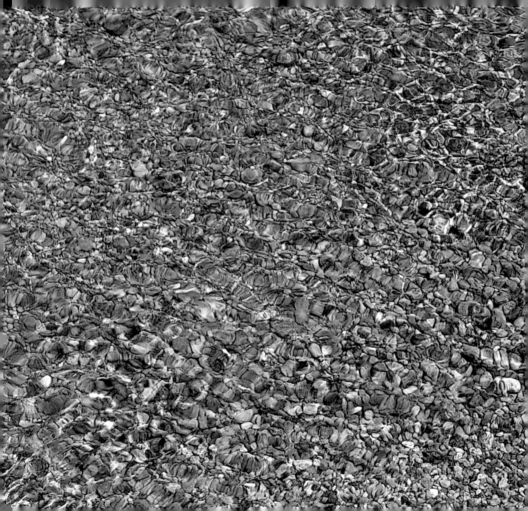

Save our front gardens!

Our enduring love affair with the car has led to off-street parking becoming increasingly popular in our cities... and the front garden becoming an endangered species. In London, it's estimated that two-thirds of front gardens are now completely or partially covered by paving, bricks or concrete – an area 22 times the size of Hyde Park!

Hard surfaces can't absorb water, so those minimalist concrete gardens are not only a flood risk, but they can also change the whole microclimate of your street and turn it into a dirtier, dustier, windier and warmer place: no greenery means less CO_2 absorption, more pollution, less wildlife; and because hard surfaces absorb more solar heat, they can turn your little patch into a heat island.

So if you're contemplating turning your front garden into a car park, think about the drainage issues. Use gravel or porous paving, which can absorb water – but if you must go for an impermeable surface, then lay it on a gradient and plant trees, shrubs and any other soft landscaping you can fit in. These simple but thoughtful measures will help solve a worsening problem – and they'll brighten your day as well as that of passers-by. Or just keep your garden and join a car club!

WATER, WATER EVERYWHERE

Without water, life on Earth wouldn't exist - but if left to its own devices, it can do untold damage to life and property. In the UK alone, more than 10,000 homes have been hit by floods in the past two years.

One way of managing water in its natural state is to plant and maintain riverside vegetation such as reed beds and grass.

These not only prevent bankside erosion, but also filter the water, slow the flow, absorb floodwater and provide valuable breeding grounds for wildlife such as the water vole, otter and bittern.

Sheepdrove Organic Farm in Lambourn, Berkshire, has installed a reedbed water treatment system which operates entirely naturally - no machinery at all is used.

It cleans and re-oxygenates used water from the farm buildings for the benefit of its livestock (including freshwater fish) and for irrigation, and it returns fully treated surplus water to the local chalk aquifer. "A significant amount of water is recycled after treatment to make savings on water consumption," says the farm, "but our main achievement is water resource conservation and recycling. We also encourage visitors, customers and other farmers to think positively about sustainable water use because with today's high demands here and all over the world, it's important to use our supplies carefully and re-use water whenever we can."

Here are some more tips:

- Fit a 'save-a-flush' bag, usually available free of charge from your water supplier, in your toilet cistern. You could save as much as 2,000 litres per person per year!
- Fix leaking taps. A dripping tap can waste up to 140 litres a week.
- When washing the car, use a couple of buckets of water (preferably from the rain butt) rather than a hosepipe.
- Don't use the washing machine until you have a full load – and use a 40°C wash cycle.
- And turn off the tap when brushing your teeth! You could save as much as 20 litres of water per day that way.

On a broader scale, we need to ensure that new housing and commercial development includes sustainable water management - effective use of rain and wastewater, and making sure that the ground is porous rather than concreted over, so that rain is soaked up and eventually reaches the underground aquifers.

And governments, too, must play their part. WWF has long argued for governments and business to increase their investments in freshwater projects not just at home, but in developing countries, too.

On average, every person on Earth needs around 25 litres of safe water a day to meet their most basic needs. So next time you ignore a dripping tap, think of the growing water crisis here at home, as well as the billion people who have to survive on contaminated water and nothing else.

SUSTAINABLE TRANSPORT

Reducing our dependence on the car

Transport. We all use it. Trains, buses, planes, cars...

Here's a statistic that may surprise you: in 1980, according to the Department for Transport, we travelled 388 billion passenger kilometres in the UK. In 2004 that had risen to 679 billion kilometres - an increase of 75%. We're getting out more, but travelling in ways which are not helping the environment.

Little wonder that transport is the fastest growing contributor to carbon dioxide emissions in the UK. Indeed, it's estimated that road transport makes up around 21% of total man-made CO_2 emissions in the UK.

So what can we do to reduce transport's Ecological Footprint? Quite a lot, as it happens.

Cars are often demonised by environmentalists, and with good reason: they pollute, they're noisy, and they burn fuel, money and our patience - especially in traffic jams. Even so, **we're not advocating a car-free future** - but we *are* saying that it's possible for us all to reduce our dependence on the car.

For example... on weekends, why not leave the car locked up and use public transport or cycle instead? If you're doing the school run, how about walking the kids there and back if it's safe, or at the very least car-sharing with other nearby parents?

My other vehicle is a Porsche!
Porsche bike, winning design Red Dot awards 2002

Then there's the interesting option of car clubs.

Car clubs are fast catching on across the UK. Members have access to a pool of vehicles which can be booked for as little as a hour and charged by time and/or mileage. They can be booked over the internet, by telephone, or even by smartcard. In effect, this is **pay-as-you-drive motoring without the worry and cost** of individual road tax, insurance, maintenance and depreciation (the average car user in the UK now spends £90 a week – that's £4,500 a year – for the privilege of driving!). And if you travel to or in London, car club vehicles are exempt from the Congestion Charge.

Once they've made the psychological leap away from private car ownership, many car club members don't want to return to the hassle of looking after their own car, but prefer having a serviced and valetted vehicle available when they need it. Some members report reducing their driving habits by as much as 90% – the single largest environmental saving in their lifestyle.

EDINBURGH - THE 'CLUB CARS' CITY

Edinburgh now has the largest city car club in the UK - and it's growing!

Here's how it works... cars are parked in reserved spaces ('car stations') all over the city close to home or work, and can be booked months ahead or at a few minutes' notice. It's a flexible and convenient solution for city people, especially those who live within a five-minute walk of a car station or for anyone who only needs a car occasionally. With some cars located at Waverley railway station, the club is now an integral part of Edinburgh's approach to sustainable transport: just one CityCarClub car replaces the need for more than five privately-owned vehicles.

If a car club isn't an option for you, another way of making large transport savings is to **opt for a more fuel-efficient vehicle** when you next change your car. Manufacturers are required to quote their new models' efficiency in terms of CO_2 released per kilometre. The difference can be enormous – look at the left-hand column of this page.

Companies such as Toyota, Honda and Ford have introduced hybrid cars. These generally use an electric motor which charges when the car is braking; the energy thus stored then assists the petrol or diesel engine when on the move.

More and more people are becoming interested in alternative fuels. One is LPG, which releases less CO_2 than an equivalent petrol engine. These days, diesel cars can run on biodiesel, a concoction made from vegetable or waste cooking oil, then mixed with ordinary diesel to protect the engine in cold weather.

Electric cars haven't been a great success so far, except in some urban areas such as central London (see page 68), where they are exempt from the Congestion Charge (as are hybrid cars). But they remain a possibility, particularly in city areas where their limited range isn't so much of a problem. (To maximise the environmental benefits of this option, it's important that the electricity used to charge them comes from renewable sources, of course.)

Public transport goes electric

G-WIZ! HOW TO AVOID THE CONGESTION CHARGE

What with the Congestion Charge and parking fees, the cost of road tax, petrol, insurance and maintenance, a growing number of Londoners are becoming more and more fed up with the hassle and expense of owning a car in the capital.

The best way of avoiding all this stress is to walk, cycle or use public transport, of course. The second best way might be to invent an eco-friendly car that's cheap to run, easy to look after and affordable to boot.

Step forward the G-Wiz! This Indian-made electric car produces near-zero emissions and is exempt from road tax and the London Congestion Charge. It can park free of charge in some parts of the city and even qualify for cheap insurance. The UK's sole G-Wiz retailer goes the extra mile and carbon-balances the emissions produced in the car's manufacture and shipping.

And what of the future? Look out for hydrogen vehicles: they're certainly clean because they generate their energy by converting hydrogen fuel into water - but as with electric vehicles, the hydrogen itself must be generated using renewable energy.

The government likes the idea of hybrid and alternatively fuelled vehicles so much that it's offering grants towards the cost of purchase. Of course, it's better not to have a car at all and join a car club - but if you really *do* need one, at least there are a range of environmental options you can now consider.

Of course, reducing car dependence often goes hand in hand with walking and cycling more. This in turn helps us build healthier lifestyles and combat the epidemic of obesity and diabetes. If we can promote communities where homes, shops, schools and offices are within walking or cycling distance, we can greatly reduce our car use. That in turn will lead to a cleaner local environment with lower levels of air pollution.

CARBON OFFSETTING

These days, we hear more and more about carbon offsetting - flying away for work or pleasure and paying into a 'green' fund as a conscience-salve. That's fine as far as it goes, but it doesn't solve the problem of our polluting behaviour. The bottom line is that we should be trying to reduce carbon emissions directly, not just polluting the atmosphere and paying to offset our actions or consciences after the fact.

First and foremost, we should be doing everything we can to reduce our emissions via energy efficiency - so cut back on those budget airline breaks, and use clean, green energy. But when we feel we can't avoid air travel, offsetting can be beneficial, so long as the scheme you choose is approved by the Gold Standard carbon credit scheme. This is owned by a network of NGOs that are committed to implementing the Kyoto protocol through emission reductions and sustainable development. (*See references page 126*)

Many people associate tree-planting with carbon offsetting but it's not a permanent solution - the trees could be burned or cut down in due course (releasing yet more CO_2 into the atmosphere), and planting them in the wrong place can change ecosystems and badly affect local biodiversity and species preservation. In any event, at the rate we're consuming resources and emitting pollutants, there wouldn't be enough room for all the trees we'd need to plant!

Air travel is an increasingly large part of our Ecological Footprint. Flying, for business and especially for holidays, is easier and cheaper than ever. Cheaper for the traveller, that is... but not for the environment. By taking one return flight to New York, you'll release as much carbon dioxide as you would driving an average car for a year. And **one return flight to Australia** will use as much as **all the energy to heat and power your home for up to six years.**

We readily acknowledge that air travel is probably the hardest area to tackle in terms of One Planet Living. We all enjoy (and work for) our overseas holidays, and tourism can be a good source of income for developing countries. But is it right that we should travel the world on untaxed aviation fuel? In effect, air travel is subsidised compared with other forms of transport.

We'd like to see aviation fuel taxed like any other fuel. The result will almost certainly be higher air fares – but in any event, the time has come to think about limiting our flying activities.

So think carefully before taking a break by air - why not take a holiday in the UK instead? And take the train, the coach or the ferry. Far more relaxing than struggling to the airport and checking in hours before that (delayed) flight!

Transport contributes about 20% to our Ecological Footprint. There are many options to reduce our dependence on the car and to use air travel more responsibly. We should aim to reduce this part of our footprint by three quarters, saving 15% of total Ecological Footprint.

- Cutting down by one long-haul flight a year could reduce your transport footprint by 24%.

- Walking or cycling for short journeys could reduce your footprint by about 4%.

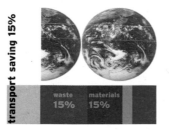

CULTURE AND HERITAGE

Best of the old and best of the new.

Culture and heritage... we all possess it and we're all a part of it. Wherever in the world we come from, each of us is defined by our background, our roots, our family, our memories, our history.

We're also defined by the home or adopted country in which we live, and by its traditions, its culture, its landscapes, towns and cities – and by its relations with other countries.

In our increasingly globalised world, culture and heritage take on an even broader perspective which embraces all manner of civilisations, languages, music, religions and ways of living. But wherever we are and whatever we do, we have one thing in common: we all share the same planet. That sharing of the planet, what we do with it and how we treat it, is at the heart of OPL's ethos and its work.

REVIVING THE ESSENCE OF TIMES PAST

Did you know that the area around Mitcham and Carshalton in south London was once the lavender-growing capital of the world? As long ago as 1749, the area's distilled lavender oil was internationally renowned for its quality. By the 1990s, however, most local people were unaware of this fragrant connection, with only the odd reference to lavender in local road names hinting at the area's illustrious past.

BioRegional, together with community groups, a local prison, the council and fragrance company Yardley has revived lavender growing and distilling by planting traditional varieties on disused land in the borough. As well as being stunning in high summer, it has helped recreate a sense of place and pride. The area now has a pub named after a local lavender harvesting family, and even its Christmas lights are based on a lavender theme.

OPL is about respecting and celebrating differences and diversity. It's about interpreting the ideas that drive it in a wide range of cultural contexts, so that each person in each community can make OPL their own by relating it to themselves and their own personal history and identity. It's all to do with creating a new local/global culture of living sustainably.

A spectacular example of that global/local culture will be the London Olympic Games in 2012. BioRegional and WWF worked closely with Sebastian Coe's team to develop a One Planet Olympics proposition, which has been cited as a key reason for London's success. The plan includes a full range of sustainable transport solutions and other energy-saving measures to ensure that the capital delivers the greenest and most sustainable Olympics the world has yet seen (see pages 82-83).

Book your tickets now!

Meanwhile, OPL offers many opportunities to revive some great local activities of the past (see *Reviving the essence of times past*). That's because we can often find great wisdom in the ways of the past and a culture which was adapted to the particular area. One of the most important expressions is found in preserving, reviving and promoting past local food traditions and culture into the future. It can also offer opportunities for us to celebrate with our local community - from cider festivals in Somerset to rhubarb-tasting in Yorkshire.

Traditional ways of using the land have sculpted the countryside we love, from the Glens of Antrim to the South Downs. In many places we're seeing a revival in rearing heritage breeds of cattle and pigs. Long-forgotten types of apple are also making a comeback.

But traditional non-food crops are worth cultivating again, too. Hemp, for example, was grown extensively across the UK. It's now gaining a new reputation because it's easy to grow organically and makes high-quality horse bedding. But let's take it further than that! We can grow it more widely as an eco-friendly source of fibres for textiles, paper, building materials and even car parts. Which means we can marry the best of the past with the best that the modern world has to offer us.

These days, our lives are enriched by modern telecommunications and the new media, bringing us instant stories, images and sounds from around the world. This same technology is now starting to support local communities in ways that we could never have imagined a generation ago.

MAIN PICTURE **hemp growing**
ABOVE **the only lasagne-based
mobile phone circuit board in the world**

Our culture and aspirations are changing
as teleworking, for example, enables remote
communities to become economically viable
and enjoy the benefits of permanent
employment.

And although their potential is largely
untapped at the moment, community
intranets and extranets will allow us all,
wherever we are, to engage more with our
neighbours, participate in local decisions
and exchange services and products locally
and beyond. Harnessing these technologies
so that they give us a sense of belonging
rather than separateness will be a vital
ingredient of OPL communities.

POLE VAULTING TO A ONE PLANET OLYMPICS

DATELINE: LONDON 2012 - a day in the life of an Olympic Athlete

I can't believe I had never even seen a pole vault when the IOC made its announcement that London was to be host city for the 2012 Games, and here I am now vying for an Olympic medal. I was still at school in Singapore at the time. I remember that the focus of everyone's attention was on my home city as the world waited to see who would win, but we were more excited about the fact that David Beckham was in town! Seven years later and London and I have grown and developed together.

The Olympic Village is the perfect place for us to relax. My coach rattles on about the need to be as conscious of our energy consumption as the buildings we're staying in are, but if I'm honest, London has been better at it than I have: the Village's energy is clean and green.

Everything's within walking distance - a bonus because cars are just an unnecessary stress and when we want to wander into town or see the sights, we get to use the team's hydrogen-powered water scooters! Most of our locally hired team equipment -

including my poles! - is made from reconstituted plastics that used to be thought of as unrecyclable and even our trainers were car tyres in a former life.

I went to meet my cousin last night who lives in east London near Bow (he considers himself a nouveau Cockney!) and I was delighted to hear that he's going to move into one of the flats in the Olympic Village in 2014 as part of the legacy developments. He's been working for the last few years as a sustainable transport consultant for the Games' organisers (thank him for the super-efficient trains right from the English Channel to your hotel bus terminus, not to mention the Olympic bikes lounging in racks for you to use at your leisure!). Soon he will be living in a home like the one I'm in now which will be warm in winter and cool in summer because of its clever mix of insulation, natural ventilation systems and local power supply - and his energy bills will be rock-bottom as well.

ZERO WASTE

Reduce, re-use, recycle – and buy recycled!

On average, each household in the UK produces over a tonne of household waste every year - that's the weight of a small car. We send as much as 80% of this to landfill... and the land's filling up. We have a crisis on our hands.

Much of what we buy comes in totally unnecessary packaging which we throw away without a second thought. And in these days of the consumer society, a fair amount of what we buy, we never keep. We often throw out things such as clothes and even furniture well before the end of their life.

It's time to *reduce* our waste, *re-use* and *repair* more, *recycle* as much as we can, and *buy more recycled* products.

ABOVE **Prototype biodegradable phone covers with implanted sunflower seeds from Warwick University**

Reducing and recycling pretty much go hand in hand because by recycling what we've used, we're reducing our waste. The trick now is to recycle locally whenever we can, and to make a point of buying recycled products (these days you can even buy pencils made from recycled polystyrene cups).

All local authorities in the UK are now required to run recycling schemes, so there's no excuse for any of us not to participate. Old newspapers and magazines, cans, bottles and even threadbare clothes are collected from our doorsteps by the local council. Some authorities collect food and garden waste, too, and turn it into compost for parks and open spaces.

But let's go back to basics – what each of us needs to do is cut back on what we use in the first place. Those supermarket plastic bags, for example. Re-use them! Better still, *never* use them! Buy a hemp bag instead – its fibres are strong and its lifelong. It will pay for itself time after time after time.

Aluminium is especially important to recycle, because its extraction from the ground and its production require huge amounts of energy. Recycled aluminium only requires 5% of the energy needed for primary production from ore (bauxite).

If you have a garden, start your own compost heap. About a third of our waste can be composted – kitchen scraps, grass cuttings and so on. If this kind of matter is thrown out and sent to landfill, it turns into methane – a potent greenhouse gas which, like CO_2, contributes to global warming.

We can also cut back on waste in our offices. Take a mug to work and stop using those polystyrene ones (even if they *can* be turned into pencils!) Recycle white paper for printing and photocopying, and persuade your company to join an office paper recycling scheme. For example, companies which have joined BioRegional's Local Paper for London scheme (*see pages 88-89*), where they recycle their waste and buy back locally recycled paper, have reduced their footprint impact from paper by 85%.

CLOSING THE LOOP - LAUNDERING LONDON'S DIRTY PAPER

What do Direct Line Insurance, the House of Commons, the Greater London Authority and the Royal Albert Hall have in common? They're all making inroads into cutting the amount of office paper that's dumped into landfill sites.

They do this through the Local Paper for London scheme. As the landfill space around London is expected to run out in five or six years, this local paper cycle scheme, which now has more than 500 offices participating, not only saves money but also helps the environment and creates jobs.

Set up by BioRegional, the scheme sends the office paper it collects to a state-of-the-art local mill for recycling, and the offices then buy the end product back again – thereby creating a closed loop. Companies are also encouraged to reduce their overall paper use, as keeping paper out of the loop in the first place is better for the pocket and the environment.

Local Paper for London has expanded recently to become The Laundry, and has launched a door-to-door collection from offices, taking away 'dirty' paper which is cleaned by the recycling process *and* delivered back as fresh paper.

Every year, Local Paper for London and The Laundry recycle around 4,300 tonnes of paper – that's the weight of some 600 double-decker buses! – that would otherwise go into landfill.

Meanwhile, here are some ideas for cutting back on your everyday waste.

Reduce

- Buy loose fruit and vegetables and avoid excess packaging.

- Reduce the amount of disposable items you buy such as tissues.

- Stop junk mail by registering with the Mailing Preference Service.

- Set your printer to print double-sided.

Re-use

- Try to re-use as much as you can in the first place.

- Utilise re-usable shopping bags.

- Donate furniture to a local homeless scheme, which will probably be able to arrange collection.

- Give good-quality unwanted clothes, toys and books to local charity shops.

- Create a tower from old tyres for growing potatoes.

- If items can't be re-used, try to recycle them instead.

Recycle

- Use your local council's kerbside collection scheme to recycle paper, glass, cans and old clothes.

- Compost your kitchen waste.

- Use local recycling sites for other items. You can often find them in supermarket car parks.

- Take larger items such as refrigerators, scrap metal and car batteries to your nearest household waste recycling centre for safe disposal.

Buy Recycled

- Office printing and photocopying paper.

- Newspaper insulation systems for cavity walls.

- Refuse sacks.

- Watering cans and garden tools.

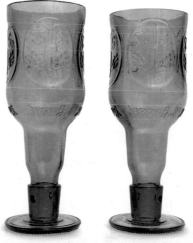

Grolsch glasses from Ecotopia

The waste we don't recycle has to be sent to landfill, incinerated or used to generate energy. Countries such as Austria and Switzerland send very little to landfill, but instead employ state-of-the-art clean 'energy from waste' technology so that the waste is put to good use.

As we move towards a more sustainable future, we'll be designing products with as much thought about what happens to them at the end of their useful life as during the time they're in use. Cars, for example, are already being designed so that they are easier to disassemble for recycling. Food packaging can now be made from vegetable matter such as maize (so-called bio-plastics) which can be composted or burned cleanly to generate renewable energy. We can make landfill a thing of the past.

In future when we buy our food, we might also be collecting material which we could use for generating electricity and heat. And the ultimate aim? To eliminate the concept of waste completely. It'll take time... but it can be done.

Waste and consumer items make up about 15% of our total Ecological Footprint.
We can each try to adopt a 'zero waste' strategy in our homes by buying goods
with less packaging, re-using and recycling wherever possible.
We should set a target to reduce this part of our footprint by two-thirds, saving
10% of our overall Ecological Footprint.

- Composting and recycling can reduce your waste footprint by as much as 40%.

- Recycling one aluminium can save enough energy to run an energy-efficient bulb for 140 hours, a computer for three hours or a television for two hours.

EQUITY AND FAIR TRADE

Local jobs and fair
international trade

It seems hard to imagine a link between an impoverished coffee farmer in Ethiopia and the frantic trading floors of the world's great international commodities markets, but it's real enough – and guess who *isn't* the winner.

Global trade in commodities such as coffee, cocoa and sugar can be every bit as volatile as in financial stocks and shares. When prices fall, losses rapidly pass down the chain to the last link – the small-scale farmer eking out a living in a developing country. At times the drop in prices has been so catastrophic that local growers from Belize to Uganda have been forced into debt, and some have lost their land and homes.

In 1986, the Max Havelaar Foundation in the Netherlands launched the first Fairtrade label for coffee sourced from Mexico. From that modest beginning has grown an organisation which now benefits half a million farmers, growers and their families – possibly five million people in all – throughout the developing world.

HEAVENLY CHOCOLATE!

In an attempt to better the wretched prices they were being paid for their cocoa bean harvest, a small group of Ghanaian farmers decided to club together in order to increase their collective bargaining power. In 1993, to get a better deal from the big chocolate companies, they set up the Kuapa Kokoo cooperative - literally translated as good cocoa farmers.

By 1997 the group - whose motto is 'pa pa paa' or 'best of the best' - decided to go one better and create their own chocolate bar. So, with support from various organisations including Comic Relief and The Body Shop, they set up The Day Chocolate Company. And so it was that the Divine chocolate bar was born.

Every Divine product carries the Fairtrade mark, which means the co-op gets a long-term trading contract and a fair price for its crop. Members are also guaranteed prompt payment, a credit union from which they can borrow money, and bonuses for good yields. The price they receive has an in-built social premium to help them improve their living and working conditions: this is achieved through community projects from new water wells to schools.

FAIRTRADE

Guarantees a **better deal** for Third World Producers

BARBECUES AND BUTTERFLIES

Coppicing is a traditional form of woodland management which has been carried out for thousands of years in Britain, but today most coppice woodlands lie neglected. Yet by using this ancient method, they can be harvested sustainably for wood, and sunny glades can be created in which woodland flowers and wildlife will thrive - including declining species such as the pearl-bordered fritillary butterfly.

Barbecue charcoal is just one of the products which can be made from coppiced wood. BioRegional coordinates a UK-wide network of

charcoal producers, each supplying local outlets of national retailers such as B&Q. By supplying locally, CO_2 from transport is reduced by more than 85% when compared with importing charcoal from tropical forests.

Think of home-grown charcoal as a 'restorative' product - when you consume it, you're helping restore wildlife habitats, maintaining an important part of our heritage and supporting local rural employment. Cook local organic produce on local charcoal and you have the perfect way of enjoying a One Planet Living summer!

Fairer trading is essential to One Planet Living: both promote social equity, justice, local economic development, decent prices and fair play. So when we're not buying locally, we should buy as much as possible that's fairly traded.

Today, brandmarked Fairtrade sales in the UK are growing rapidly and the accent is on quality. Fairtrade Labelling Organisations International (FLO) sets international standards and monitors the whole range of Fairtrade products. These include Ghanaian cocoa, Nicaraguan coffee, Chilean honey, Indian tea, Paraguayan sugar and bananas from the Windward Islands. Producers registered with FLO receive a minimum price that covers the cost of production and an extra premium that's invested in the local community.

But what about people here in the UK? After all, fair trade is as important as Fairtrade - and the buying and selling of local goods and produce is an important part of OPL communities. Whether from the Windward or the Shetland Islands, it's the investment in *people* that counts - but so, too, does consideration for the environmental impact of our purchasing decisions.

Equity - access and opportunity for all - is also a central part of the OPL ethos. It's unacceptable that because someone is disabled, of a minority persuasion, or socially disadvantaged in some respect, they should be denied access to everyday courtesies and facilities that are taken for granted by most people.

All OPL communities (see page 120) will be committed not only to providing affordable housing, but also to reducing local unemployment through a job and training plan for any resident who needs help. Access for disabled people to all buildings, services, open areas and transport systems is a priority, as is the provision of community spaces with multi-faith halls for all who want them.

And finally, back to fair trade and Fairtrade... each OPL community will offer trading concessions to both types of outlet - so there won't be far to go for your home-grown groceries and your tea, coffee and bananas from a little further afield!

SUSTAINABLE MATERIALS

Buy recycled or sustainable products and help enhance the natural world

What have a mouse mat, a doll's house, a set of wine glasses, a pencil and concrete got in common? The answer is that they can all be made from recycled material. These, and hundreds more items, are easily found in catalogues and on the internet as recycling becomes more and more popular. And with good reason - not only has the quality of the products increased enormously in recent years, but recycling is also an important part of One Planet Living.

MAIN PICTURE **Cyclotron guitar designed by Simon Lee, in Double Espresso, produced from vending machine coffee cups**

Here in the UK, government and industry are investing heavily in developing even greater ranges of recycled products. Paper goods from tissues to quality notepaper are already common – and recycling is becoming such an accepted way of life that we're often using recycled products without knowing. For example, a lot of chipboard now contains recycled wood.

RECYCLING WITH A SMILE

Worried about what happens to some of those 'unrecyclables' that get thrown out... the old wellington boots and cracked CDs, for example? Well, innovative design company Smile recycles all sorts of weird and wonderful things – including washing up bottles, throw-away coffee cups, crisp packets and even mobile phones. All this and more is turned into durable products ranging from kitchen worktops to funky electric guitars. Projects like this divert waste from landfill to create useful and eye-catching products which we can all enjoy.

ABOVE, RIGHT **Re-form chair by Aaron Moore from PLI Designs and Smile Plastics for the Eden Project Café A great example of closed loop recycling – backs and seats of all the chairs are made from plastic cups used at the Eden Project.**

Recycled DIY and garden products are also becoming more and more popular. Crushed green glass sand, recycled aggregates, reclaimed timber, bricks and even

steel joists are now readily available, as is compost made from green waste. Indeed, many local authorities now make and sell this compost, and it's also on sale in some garden centres and DIY stores.

But there's more to OPL than recycling. Sustainably managed natural products and locally sourced materials also have a crucial part to play in our everyday lives. By using local products we can cut down on transport costs, CO_2 emissions and our Ecological Footprint – and in many cases, enhance and beautify the area we live in. What can be more pleasing to the eye than villages built from local stone in the Cotswolds or the Lake District?

Then there's the question of timber. The world's forests are still under constant attack from illegal and destructive logging, plantation expansion, forest conversion, fragmentation and other threats, so buying timber products that come from legal and sustainable sources is vital to conservation. These days, you can buy almost any wood product from a forest that has been checked and verified. Look out for the Forest Stewardship Council label on everything from garden gates to key rings – the FSC 'tick-tree' symbol guarantees it's from a well-managed source.

You might also buy wood products that come from a local woodland or forest, where you'll be able to see for yourself how it's being managed (this will be a good way of supporting local rural employment as well). Some woodland products – barbecue charcoal and firewood, for example – come from wood harvested through the traditional technique of coppicing (see *Barbecues and butterflies* on pages 98-99).

BUYING TIMBER PRODUCTS WITH CONFIDENCE

Next time you're out shopping for a timber product, look out for the Forest Stewardship Council (FSC) 'tick-tree' label.

The FSC is a non-profit organisation which independently verifies good forest management. It provides credible tracking of products from forest to consumer and guarantees that those carrying its 'tick-tree' label come from well-managed forests.

Co-founded by WWF, the FSC has the support of other environmental organisations, unions, indigenous people, private, communal and state forest owners, timber industries and scientists in over 60 countries. It offers the only worldwide certification system for good forest management.

Because no country on Earth can allow the wealth of its forests to be squandered, FSC certification is more important than ever.

ABOVE, LEFT Rod Waterfield, woodland worker, North Wales

And what about textiles? Although a natural fibre, **cotton is one of the most damaging crops in the world:** cotton production requires large quantities of fresh water, pesticides and herbicides and has caused serious environmental and health problems. Where water is in short supply, even organically grown cotton can be a matter of concern. So think before buying

Hemp jacket (above) and Herdwick sheep

cotton, then go for organic products – but do also consider wool, flax and hemp, because all these can be produced at a lower cost to the environment. Then there are fabrics such as Lyocell, a new fibre made from natural cellulose that's similar to rayon. Whenever we buy local, sustainable or recycled products, we're helping to enhance the natural world around us. It's easy to do... and it doesn't cost the earth.

● Materials used for building our homes, making our clothes and furniture and constructing roads and airports contributes about 15% to our total Ecological Footprint. By reclaiming, recycling and buying local and low-impact products, we could reduce this to 5%.

materials saving 10%

HEALTH AND HAPPINESS

Go for the simple things in life – they are footprint-free

So... can saving the planet actually make you happier? And healthier? All too often environmentalists are seen as doom-mongers. Rainforests are disappearing, holes in the ozone layer are a continuing problem, sea levels are rising and low-lying places are going to flood because of climate change. While all this is true, and most of us do care about these things, they can make for pretty depressing reading.

Does anyone get up in the morning and think, 'I'll go and destroy a rainforest today', or 'I think I'll deprive some poor people in another part of the world of a decent living'? It's unlikely. But the reality is that all of our daily decisions and actions *do* have an impact, good or bad, on other people and nature. The problem for most of us is that it's all too easy to make decisions that have negative effects, and often it seems more difficult, or expensive, to do what's right. But things are changing, and we can all help make them change more quickly.

Giants' Causeway

If you ask someone what's most important to them and their family, the chances are they'll mention health and happiness. Every day we work hard to achieve these things. We strive to earn more money to buy things we like and to make life more enjoyable. We go on holiday so that we can relax and come back looking and feeling healthier and happier. And who can blame us? The point is, most of us have choices, and OPL enables us to think about the consequences of different choices. Will doing or buying something really give us what we want, or make us feel the way we want to feel?

In fact, health, happiness and saving the planet can go together rather well. Eating a balanced diet, with seasonal vegetables produced without toxic chemicals, makes us healthier. And by buying local produce, we can feel good about supporting our farming neighbours. By improving the insulation in our homes, we feel warmer and cosier in winter, and we also feel a lot happier when the bills come through the letterbox in the spring!

When we decide to walk to the shops, or cycle, we get a bit of exercise and fresh air, and sometimes see things we wouldn't normally notice when we speed by in our car. We might bump into a friend or neighbour, have a chat, and feel more in touch with our local community.

The problem is that many of the things we've become accustomed to in our daily lives were invented at a time when people didn't have to think about the Earth's limited resources. People thought that everything the planet gave us was free and limitless, like the air we breathe. But now we've reached a point, with a global population of 6.3 billion and set to rise to 7.5 billion by 2020, where we've realised there isn't actually enough to keep us all in the manner to which we in the affluent West have become accustomed. As we said at the beginning of this book, if everyone lived as we do today in the UK, we'd actually need three planets to support us all.

IN PURSUIT OF GROSS NATIONAL HAPPINESS

For some years now, economists have been looking for a more reliable way to measure our quality of life than Gross National Product (GNP). One surprising source of inspiration is the little-known country of Bhutan, a kingdom about the size of Switzerland, high in the eastern Himalayas. In 1998 the King told his people that as far as his government was concerned, 'Gross National Happiness' (GNH) was more important than Gross National Product!

The King (right) believes that as happiness is the most common goal of his people, both individually and collectively, public policies based on GNH will be far less arbitrary than those based on standard economic tools.

Could such a radical departure be seen here in the UK? Well, in 2002 the Cabinet Office held a string of 'life satisfaction seminars' and the Prime Minister's Strategy Unit published a paper recommending policies to increase the nation's happiness.

Of course, for people who don't have enough to eat, or a decent home to shelter from the elements, more goods and services are essential and entirely desirable. But for the rest of us, there is increasing evidence that the benefit we get from having and consuming more actually reduces (certainly in terms of our sense of happiness and wellbeing) the more we have.

For many years, economists and governments around the world have used Gross National Product (GNP) as a measure of our prosperity, and have linked this directly to our quality of life. The trouble is that those things measured don't necessarily make us happy. GNP may include the cost of cleaning up an oil spill at sea, because this involves all kinds of economic activity - hardly a contribution to our quality of life or sense of wellbeing!

If we apply the philosophy of OPL, we're likely to appreciate our surroundings more. By growing and eating seasonal produce, for example, we become more aware of the changing seasons and the effects on plants and wildlife in our gardens, or our local parks and woodlands. More and more of us live in smaller family units (indeed many live alone), yet we crave a sense of community. In South-east England there are now huge waiting lists for allotments, which have been rediscovered as a source of social interaction as well as an extension to our outside space for food growing. Farmers' markets are fighting back against the big supermarkets, because they make food shopping fun and different again - we like to chat to stallholders who make their own chutney or rear their own pigs.

GETTING FIT - THE GREEN WAY!

Want to get fit? If going to the gym or a sports centre doesn't appeal to you, try a Green Gym instead - a chance to work out in the open air on a practical conservation project. After some basic warming-up exercises with trained leaders, you could find yourself planting a new hedge or helping to build a community garden. According to BTCV,  which runs the Green Gym programme, almost a third more calories can be burned in an hour than in a step aerobics class! No previous experience or equipment is needed, just some old clothes and a willing heart - and all sessions are free. Green Gyms meet once a week for up to three hours, and activities are conducted at your own pace. There are 70 BTCV Green Gym projects throughout the UK, so there may well be one near you. Go to www.btcv.org.uk to find out!

We don't have to live in remote Himalayan kingdoms to be happier and healthier. But nor do we always have to buy the latest electronic gadget or succumb to the supermarket promotion of air-freighted strawberries in December in the pursuit of happiness. When was the last time you felt really happy, or healthy for that matter? The chances are that the things that really made you feel that way – laughing with friends, or seeing that sensational panoramic view – were *really* very simple and didn't cost the Earth. Happiness is good for us – a fact proven by the medical profession in case we didn't already know it. Happier people tend to live longer, have better immune systems, lower levels of stress, and lower blood pressure. One Planet Living is as good for us as it is for the environment!

TAKE A HOLIDAY WITH ONE PLANET LIVING

BioRegional and WWF are helping to develop a network of OPL communities around the world to demonstrate that it really is possible for people everywhere to enjoy a good standard of living within their fair share of the Earth's resources. OPL communities will encompass not only good-quality homes and offices, but also schools, shops, health and leisure amenities, and strong transport and food links.

Plans for OPL communities are under way in Australia, China, North America, Portugal and South Africa, as well as here in the UK.

In Portugal, the Mata de Sesimbra residential and eco-tourism project near Lisbon is being planned and developed according to the OPL principles you've been reading about in this book. It will create the world's first integrated sustainable building, tourism, nature conservation and reforestation programme, with a total investment of more than €1 billion. Ultimately, the development will become an 'eco-city' for up to 30,000 people. Final planning permission is awaited and it's hoped building work may begin before the end of 2006. Meanwhile, nearly 1,200 acres (480 hectares) of the surrounding area - a mixture of disused sand quarries, clay pits and introduced pine and eucalyptus plantations - have already been restored through replanting native trees, such as cork, oak and umbrella pine, and other conservation work.

LEFT **Prototype eco-house in Portugal**

And finally...

As you near the end of this book, you will by now have discovered that One Planet Living has its eye firmly on the future, and a *sustainable* future at that.

It's humbling to think how much we still have to learn – but it's exciting, too. In many respects, the technological revolution has only just begun. Whoever had heard of the internet 20 years ago – and where will it lead us? The quality of electronic communications is outstanding compared with just 10 years ago. And the rapid advances in medical care seem boundless (although who would have thought that a major player in the treatment of child leukaemia would be found in the rosy periwinkle, a pretty flowing plant found in the tropical forests of Madagascar?)

The answer to that last question is... local people. We talk more and more about the world's tropical forests being the 'medicine chests of the future' – but people indigenous to those places have understood the wealth of their natural surroundings for millennia.

What *we* have to understand is our responsibility to make sure that the natural wonders of the world remain intact and flourish, for the good of us all.

By working with local people to build a worldwide network of OPL communities we believe we can learn from one another, enhance people's lives and the health of those natural wonders and the world around us.

One of our OPL commitments is to gather and interpret the latest information relating to our Ecological Footprint and to track solutions that will benefit ourselves and future generations, wherever they may be.

And it's to those future generations that we look. They have the great benefits of time and undreamed-of technology on their side – and that's just as well because the challenges they will face may well be more daunting that our own. So if the children of today are to overcome the environmental challenges of tomorrow, introducing them to the concept of OPL right now is a very good start: awareness achieves wonders.

One way of familiarising school children and students with the environment is to enable them, through their lessons and everyday activities, to make connections between themselves and their physical and social surroundings – for example, the links between their school or college, its environment and the community, based on OPL principles.

To encourage critical thinking among young people is, we believe, vital. Armed with that approach, they can analyse their surroundings and devise positive changes so that the goal of living sustainably becomes a reality. This participation in decision-making will also have the important side-effect of building their skills and confidence so that they can make sound choices in their adult lives.

Today, more than ever, each of us has to think about what we as *individuals* can do to help protect the Earth and its natural resources. Some of us work in government, some in business, others have the full-time job of raising children and taking care of our families. We all have a contribution to make. In the end we only have one planet Earth, and it's home to us all. The more we embrace One Planet Living, the greater our contribution will be to the wellbeing of the Earth and the future generations who will inhabit it. What greater legacy could we leave?

REFERENCES

One Planet Living oneplanetliving.org
BioRegional bioregional.com
WWF-UK wwf.org.uk

BTCV btcv.org.uk
British Wind Energy Association bwea.com
Carbon Trust thecarbontrust.co.uk
CityCar Club (Smart Moves) citycarclub.co.uk
Divine chocolate, The Day Chocolate Company divinechocolate.com
Duke of Cambridge organic pub sloeberry.co.uk
Defra defra.gov.uk
Department for Transport dft.gov.uk
Duchy Home Farm at Highgrove duchyoriginals.com
Ecological Footprint ecologicalbudget.org.uk
Ecotopia ecotopia.co.uk
Energy Saving Trust est.org.uk
Fairtrade Foundation fairtrade.org.uk
Fragile Earth books fragile-earth.com
G-Wiz goingreen.co.uk
Gold Standard carbon credits cdmgoldstandard.org
Green roofs livingroofs.org
Low Carbon Vehicle Partnership lowcvp.org.uk
Mailing Preference Service mpsonline.org.uk
Marine Stewardship Council msc.org
National Association of Farmers Markets farmersmarkets.net
Rainforest Alliance rainforest-alliance.org
Renewable Energy Foundation ref.org.uk
Renewable Energy Systems res-ltd.com
Sheepdrove Organic Farm Sheepdrove.com
Smile Plastics smile-plastics.co.uk see also simonleeguitars.com and plidesign.co.uk
Soil Association soilassociation.org
WaterAid wateraid.org

A NOTE FROM OUR SPONSOR, BIOREGIONAL QUINTAIN

"OPL is part of our DNA,"
Pete Halsall, Managing Director, BioRegional Quintain Ltd.

"Here is a view of what One Planet Living can look like. As a leading UK property developer, we have teamed up with BioRegional to design and build communities across the UK incorporating all ten One Planet Living principles. This is an early image of one of them - Middlehaven in Middlesbrough - which we aim to start constructing in 2007. Overleaf are our proposals for New England Quarter in Brighton, where it will be easy for people to adopt a one-planet lifestyle without compromising their desire for fun and a high quality way of life."
Nick Shattock, Property Director, Quintain Estates and Development PLC